MW01712537

Reflections

A COLLECTION OF POEMS
& WRITINGS

Christopher P. Obert

Reflections...

A collection of poems & writings

Published by Obert Publishing
Bradford, Massachusetts 01835
ObertPublishing@att.net

❖

First Edition

❖

Proudly printed in the United States of America
By Signature Book Printing, Inc. Gaithersburg, MD
To order additional copies and other great books, visit
Signature Book's bookshelf page at www.signature-book.com

Obert, Christopher P.
Reflections, a collection of poems & writings / by Christopher P. Obert. – 1st Ed.

ISBN 0-9749291-1-5
Library of Congress Control Number: 2005900083

1. American Poetry - Author 2. Poetry – Interpret 3. Love Poetry
I. Title II. Obert, Shari

Author's Photograph by Nancy Obert
Cover & Book Design by Christopher P. Obert
Images supplied by Art Explosion 600,000 -
Nova Development Corporation Copyright © 1995-98

Dedication

To Love
and all of its forms;

and

to everyone I have
shared my love with...

Table of Contents:

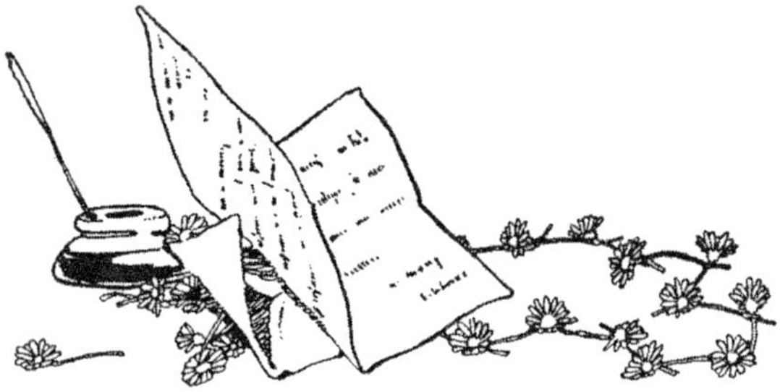

People and Places

My Wife and Children

Thoughts and Emotions

Faith

People and Places

"Good writing excites me, and makes life worth living."
- Harold Pinter

The Hill

❖

Home is more than a location,
it is a state of mind.
As there can be only one true love,
there can be only one true home.
To everyone it is the same,
not the setting, but the emotion.
For me, home is the hill
where I was born, grew, played and loved.
It is woven into my being,
just as I am a part of its soil.
Although I have been away longer than I was there,
it knows I never left.
In my dreams
I still visit the paths and streets of the past.
Today the people living there do not know me,
but the hill knows me.
The hill is a part of me and I a part of it,
and my spirit walks free.

❖

Me

❖

I am.
At least, I think I am!

I live.
I walk, I talk, I play.

I dream.
I remember the times I've had
and reach for the days ahead.

I sing.
My heart beats with happiness and sorrow.

I love.
For those close to me are inside of me.

I believe.
There is more to me than meets the eye.

I trust.
I am part of the universe,
and it is a part of me.

I am!
And there are billions of "Me's"…

❖

Good-bye, My Friend

Death's sting is harsh and cold
It seeks out both,
The young and the old

It robs us of our freedom
It blinds us of our sight
It often causes us to act
Wrong-doing not right

Its reach is all encompassing
This Romeo and Hamlet know
Reaching king and servant equally
Causing many a tear to flow

Death is relentless
Invincible, stubborn yet fair
Taking that which belongs to each
The hated, the lost, the dear

It can put an end to misery
By opening it's door so wide
Whether the well or the sick
For none of us could hide

Not man, nor beast, nor empire
For each will have it's time
And they will know it is done
When the clock begins to chime

For death has visited many before
And this won't be the last
Of all of life's great mysteries
It is the hardest one to grasp

For its power comes from God above
And He knows what is right
But I understand it not
On this cold and lonely night

At Home (Strolling Through Time)

❖

As I stroll through downtown Haverhill, the years and minutes pass.
I start in one of the commons, and walk among the grass.

I want to see all the sights and scenes, or at least I want to try.
I want to meet every face, was that George Washington that passed by?

I told Hannah to be careful, and Isaac Roberts to have a safe trip.
The day was getting hot, so I stopped at Plug's Pond for a dip.

I went into Bailey's Drug Store, to get something to drink.
Edward Capen brought me to the reading room, so I could sit and think.

Past the Griffin House, Gardner House, and the Daggett Building went thee.
The view from the top of Tilton's Tower was quite impressive to see.

Duncan's eagle looked down at me, as the snow roller passed by
The snow covers all the streets, so I give tobogganing a try.

The February snow is melted away, by a great fire the next day.
But the Queen City will go on, that's what the people say.

The residents here are true, they always extended a hand.
Their kindness resonates across the streets, river and land

I paused at Kenoza, and looked across the Lake,
Its mirror surface broken, by the passing of a drake.

I climb the hill to the Winnekenni Castle ground,
A herd of peaceful deer is what I quickly found.

What a lovely trip, it has been like a dream.
Should I contact someone and tell them what I've seen?

Should I send a message from the Western Union Telegraph,
Or should I send an e-mail, which would be the better draft?

I think I'll ponder and sit, and try to write a poem,
To allow them to see the beauty, and to make them feel at home.

❖

Not Everyone Can Be a Poet

❖

Trying to write a poem
I know what I want to say
The poem should be about my wife and kids
Although the words are not coming today.

I want to share my feelings
I want to relive our past
I know when this writer's block breaks
I'll have to write it down fast.

Not everyone can write a poem
And my block is here to stay
I will have to do what others do
And just love them every day…

❖

Chris' Law

❖

How can you enjoy someone else's happiness,

at the price of your own?

❖

On a Corner Street

❖

My heart stood hollow

Following love's quiet death

Days turn to years searching for comfort

❖

My Wife and Children

"The right reader of a good poem can tell the moment it strikes him that he has taken an immortal wound – that he will never get over."
- Robert Frost

December and You

❖

December's glow is cool and clean,
Its power comes from a Christmas Dream.
It's the season of winter, the season of white,
December shines of star filled nights…
December gives of unparalleled lengths.
She's given me presents of Beauty and Strength.
She's given a treasure the mind can't conceive.
December's given love that I still can't believe.
December means more,
Than the bright blazing sun,
Because it was that mystical month,
That we became one!

❖

An Open Letter to Y3K

❖

Nancy,

I just want to tell you that, if I live to see the year 3000 I will never find another like YOU. I have thought about the year 2000 so many times when I was young. What the world would be like, what would I be like. I thought about so many things. But, I never thought of someone like you standing next to me. It's funny now that we are here...2000... and the only thing I can think of is YOU. I will always thank God that he brought us together and I will always love you and the kids. So until the year 3000 comes around and we do it all over again,

I love you and want to wish you a Very Happy New Year.

Chris

❖

A Picture

❖

There was the one, who damaged my body,
There was one, that threatened my soul,

But there is only one I want beside me,
As I am growing old!

I want her beside me, in good times and in bad.
Because I love her more,
Than any other that I ever had.

If you want to know the person
I want with me all my life.

Just ask me, and I'll show you
A picture…

A picture of my wife!

❖

The Lady and the Children

❖

No one can understand how I feel.
Can mere words describe this thing called love?
I know what it means when it is real,
But can the soul be free as a dove?
More yes than no, for my soul does sail,
Because you are much more than a dream.
Will true love be our endless tale?
As forever becomes our life's theme.
One December my lady and me,
Joined our love and became like one.
No matter what happens you will see,
Although rain will fall, still mostly sun.
Starting a new chapter, time moves on,
Happiness and the larger family tree.
Place the children's voices in our song.
Look, our souls are truly at last free.
I know my dream came true…
Because of my children and you!

❖

Please Don't Ever Go

❖

It's gone but not forgotten
Life's worth rebuilding
Days are over now
Love's worth is sharing

Time has changed the faces
Feelings are growing
The world is still revolving
Spinning slowly on

Please don't ever leave me
Please don't ever go
My love for you is building
In time we'll watch it grow

My song of love is simple
I'll say it once again
I need your love and caring
To get me through the end

Please don't ever leave me
Please don't ever go
My love for you is building
In time we'll watch it grow

Please don't ever leave me
Please don't ever go
I need your love and caring
Please Don't Ever Go…

❖

The Unending Love Game

❖

Two children happened to me
So I can rarely rest
Still God I thank Thee
For I am truly blessed

Because I rarely rest
I have time to watch them grow
For which I am truly blessed
Although the time does flow

As I watch them grow
I learn from them each day
Quickly the time does flow
I don't know what to say

I learn from them each day
There's more to life than me
I don't know how to say
It's better to be 'We'

I will never be the same
And God I thank Thee
For this unending game
For two children happened to me

❖

Thoughts and Emotions

"You can't blame a writer for what the characters say."
- Truman Capote

Stephanie – Broken Dream Girl

❖

Stephanie won't you come with me…

I could make your dreams come true

Stephanie won't you come to me…

Can't you see that I love you?

You and me, Yah we didn't see
Broken Dream Girl
Me for you and you for me
Broken Dream Girl

Though the days were good and the nights were better

I still die and cry when I read your letter

'Cause I knew our love couldn't get no better

Broken Dream Girl

You need to run, Yah you need to be free
Broken Dream Girl
You locked your heart and I lost the key
Broken Dream Girl

In the shadows you just drift away

In the night-time all you do is play

And your courage and strength just slip away

Broken Dream Girl

When you're lonely and you finally see
Broken Dream Girl
Don't come running, don't come looking for me
Broken Dream Girl

When it's late at night and you're all alone

And you call me up girl I'm not at home

'Cause that's what it's like to be left alone

Broken Dream Girl

❖

Rake the Dead

❖

Hollywood Star – shining above,
Blazing on the silver screen.
Using her body – licking her lips,
She makes the old men scream.
Climbing the ladder – makes her feel hotter,
Steppin' on other's dreams.
Looking for rivals – she's a bitch from heaven,
Tears them apart at the seams.

Rake – Rake the Dead
Rake, she rapes the dead

Everyone's passion – makes her feel wanted,
Not happy with what she sees.
The living legend – destroying all others,
Rupturing past stars deeds.
Corporate author – of scandalous rumors,
Dirty graves are what she needs.
Convincing the others – with acts of pleasure,
She gets down on her knees.

Rake – Rake the Dead
Rake, she rapes the dead

Burning up lovers – devouring their treasures,
Has taken its toll it seems.
Filling her veins - with acid and liquor,
Her body and soul just scream.
Buried her in – her gold and leather,
They covered her with white fur.
But she can't sleep nice - In Hollywood's heaven,
Cause now they rake her…

Rake – Rake the Dead
Rake, they rape the dead!

❖

Seafarer's Cabin

❖

Broken buoys on the porch - Hard wooden floor
Bell on the hook - Sturdy carved door
Old books on a shelf - Maps and charts galore
Old organ in the corner - Hard wooden door
Old picture on the wall - Sturdy carved floor
Warm blanket on the bed - Who could ask for more?

Ship in a bottle - Hard wooden floor
Flour in a jar - Sturdy carved door
Pen and paper on the desk - Maps and charts galore
Hymnals on the mantel - Hard wooden door
Bless this Home on the wall - Sturdy carved floor
With his wife in the bed - Who could ask for more?

❖

Before It's Too Late

❖

Unfortunately, not senseless love

But wasted time

Are found in the depths below

❖

The Unsaid Word

❖

Moments beyond understanding

transported friendship unprepared for love.

❖

Timeless

❖

The sun, moon and planets will certainly end

But our true love is safe

For heaven is beyond time.

❖

Music

❖

His desire found silence in his voice

Hands soft then hot slowly learned to release

Fingers touch and praise Ludwig

❖

Desperation

❖

Inaudible logic cries desperation

Muting shadows burning velvet desire

Diffusing the soul's breathless dream

Obscuring passionate whispers and delicious thoughts.

❖

Past Memories

❖

Tenderly I take the page

The love within the message unlocks my soul

For these words found joy.

❖

Oblivious

❖

Her desire Her wonder Her love

She passes She never stays

She is beloved

For I love her

❖

Memories

❖

When dusty memories

Saddened by buried love

Become forgotten wounds

Waking souls, once tired, roam free…

❖

Snowflakes – On the River of Time

❖

Each moment of our lives
Is like a snowflake,
Special, with no two alike.

This collection of countless moments,
Each a sparkling gem,
Combine to assemble a crystal web,
That is unique to each of us.

Over the course of our lives,
These snowflakes
Build to create the body of our soul.

Memories fade and
Time melts away some of those layers,
Only to be rebuilt with the next snowfall.

And each of us is likewise a snowflake,
One building upon another
Combining to create a river of snow

Forever flowing…

❖

Faith

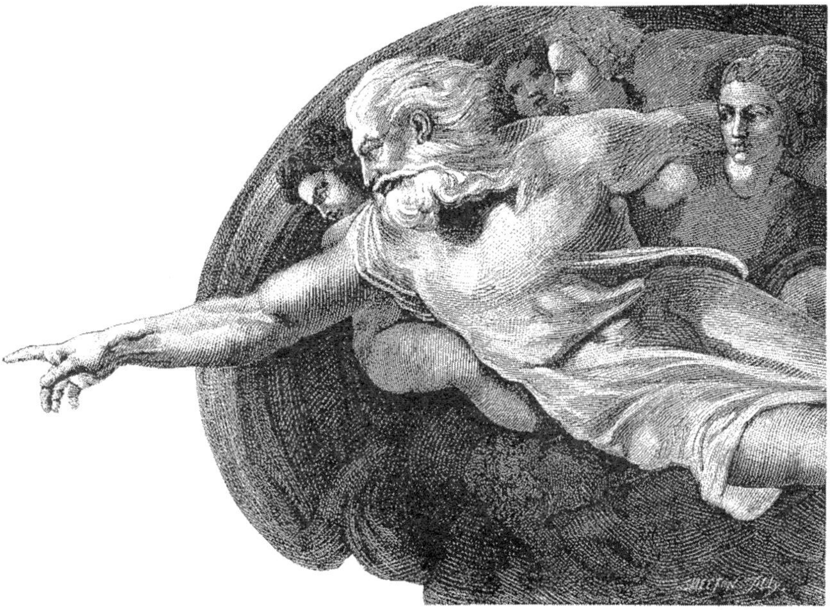

"The poet is the priest of the invisible."
- Wallace Stevens

God and Religion

❖

God is like the sun,
and religion it's reflection.
Depending on the point of view of the observer,
the reflection may be
a single streak or a multitude.
It may have a dull luster
or the brilliance of the rainbow
and all of its colors.
But it is not the reflection that matters,
or the belief that it is seen at all.

What does matter is the truth
in the fact
that the sun does shine…

❖

Chris' Prayer

❖

Dear God

Thank You for all the gifts You have given me:
My life, my family and my friends
and the wonderful world around us.
My prayer to You is that
I may be worthy of these gifts and that
the world and I remain a loving part of Your creation.

❖

God the Artist

❖

You are a masterpiece

Soft laugh   delicious colors

Painful desire   silky hot

Closed eyes   open love

Behold God the Artist

❖

Nature's King

❖

God's unending heaven

'Tis enduring winter and beloved spring

Hence life and death could not end

❖

To Touch the Universe

❖

Each life bridges time.

Resonating hope.

Whose soft and silky love

Build oneness to the universe.

❖

Crucified

❖

Society Searching   Souls Feel

Minds Desire   Pity Found

Love Granted   Life Altered

❖

War and Liberty

"Whatever sentence will bear to be read twice,
we may be sure was thought twice."
- Henry David Thoreau

Planets of War

❖

Down a long tube in a land afar…
A child looks out at a distant star.
As he looks out over miles of open space,
A look of disgrace comes over his face.
As the men of that world toy with their life,
Soon to be killed by the edge of a knife.
What silly things these Earthlings be…
To throw away the only key!
Even with their certain fate,
They never try to change that date.
For it eventually must come
To worlds that are so dumb;
They enter Death's only door,
Such is the fate of Planets of War.

❖

America

❖

Treasure found through liberty

Penetrates the shackled dungeon of uncertainty

With dreams of opportunity

The Promise of Freedom Beckons…

❖

When Will We Learn

❖

Silently death laughs when

War's inevitable ashes kill love

Suddenly wounded ghosts embrace waste

❖

Eternal Dream

❖

Enduring cold night
Lost souls scream
Gates of Babylon in sight

Heroes desert in fright
War's unending scheme
Enduring cold night

Fire burning bright
Blood and sword gleam
Gates of Babylon in sight

Lonely fallen knight
Decaying bodies steam
Enduring cold night

War's evil might
Misery the theme
Gates of Babylon in sight

Endless human blight
Death's eternal dream
Enduring cold night
Gates of Babylon in sight

❖

The Words of War

❖

Abortion, Absurdity, Aggression, Alcohol, Alienation, Anarchy, Anger, Argument, Arrogance, Aspiration, Association, Atheism, Authority, Behavior, Belief, Betrayal, The Bible, Bigotry, Blindness, Boasting, Boldness, Bribery, Bureaucracy, Business, Capitalism, Captivity, Censorship, Change, Chaos, Charm, Choice, Christianity, Church, Circumstance, Civil Rights, Class, Closed-Mindedness, Communication, Communism, Competition, Conflict, Conformity, Confusion, Contempt, Corruption, Courage, Cowardice, Cruelty, Cults, Cunning, Danger, Death, Debauchery, Debt, Decline, Defense, Democracy, Dependence, Deprivation, Desires, Despair, Destiny, Destruction, The Devil, Difficulty, Discovery, Discrimination, Dishonesty, Disillusionment, Distrust, Divorce, Drugs, Economics, Education, Effort, Ego, Emotions, Enemies, Envy, Equality, Events, Evil, Evolution, Exaggeration, Excess, Excuses, Expectation, Exploration, Failure, Faith, Family, Fascism, Fate, Faults, **Fear**, Feminism, Fighting, The Flag, **Food**, Force, Foreigners, Freedom, Frustration, Gambling, Glory, God, Gossip, Government, Greatness, **Greed**, Growth, Guns, Haste, Hate, Heaven, Hell, Heroes, History, Homeland, Homosexuality, **Honor**, Horror, Hunger, Hypocrisy, Idealism, Ideas, Identity, Ideology, Idleness, Ignorance, Illusion, Imitation, Immaturity, Impatience, Incompetence, Indecision, Indifference, Indignation, Indulgence, Inequality, Inevitability, Inferiority, Inflation, Ingratitude, Injury, Injustice, Insincerity, Insults, Intolerance, Invention, Involvement, Irritation, Islam, **Jealousy**, Jews, Journalists, Judgment, Justice, Killing, Knowledge, Language, Laughter, Laws, Laziness, Leaders, Liberalism, Lies, Literacy, Losers, Love, Loyalty, **Lust**, Madness, Malice, Manners, Marriage, Martyrs, Materialism, Meanness, Mediocrity, Memory, The Military, Minority, Misery, **Mistakes**, Monarchs, Money, Motives, Mysticism, Myth, Nationalism, Necessity, Neighbors, Neutrality, News, Nobility, Noise, Nonsense, Nuclear Weapons, Obedience, Obligation, Opinions, Opportunity, Opposition, Oppression, Order, Pain, Passion, The Past, Patriotism, Perception, Pessimism, The Police, Politics, Pollution, Population, Pornography, Poverty, **Power**, Preachers, Prejudice, Pride, Principle, Prisons, Privacy, Propaganda, Property, Prophecy, Protest, Punishment, Race, Racism, Radicalism, Rank, Rape, Rebellion, Recession, Reciprocity, Reform, **Religion**, Respect, Responsibility, Revenge, Revolution, Reward, Right, Safety, Sanity, Science, Secrets, Selfishness, Sin, Slander, Slavery, Socialism, Society, Solidarity, Sorrow, The Soul, Space, Sports, Stealing, Stubbornness, Stupidity, Superiority, Superstition, Survival, Taxes, Temper, Terrorism, Theology, Threat, Totalitarianism, Tradition, Trust, Truth, Ugliness, Unemployment, Unhappiness, Unions, The Unknown, Value, Vanity, Violence, Voting, Water, Wealth, **Words**…

❖

Nature

"The difference between the right word and the almost right word is the difference between lightning and the lightning bug."
- Mark Twain

Dreaming of Spring

❖

The days fly

Stringing delicious memories

Of silky rain, steady sun

Fallen leaves and damp snow

Wildflowers harvested, leaves turning

Specters dark against the tree

Another dark dormant winter

Desiring an early spring

❖

The Harmony of the Birch

❖

All the colors
Live in peace
On the birch tree

Black and white on the trunk
Red and green on the leaf
Brown and gold at the birch's feet

All the colors
Live in peace
On the birch tree

Silver snow on the trunk
Yellow sun on the leaf
Blue water at the birch's feet

All the colors
Live in peace
On the birch tree

They live in harmony
With each other
Yet each of them still free

All the colors
Live in peace
On the birch tree
Likewise - Why can't we?

❖

The Wind Chime

❖

Blocks of wood
Lengths of metal
How effortlessly you sway

Links of chain
Lengths of wire
You bring music to my day

String of notes
Lengths of breeze
How sweet the tune you play

❖

Across the Sea

❖

Cool white fog glides across the sea
As the rusted anchor whispers its story
The sailing gulls sing their sad song
As the gentle breeze sways the dory

Countless ripples stroll across the sea
As the mist is parted by the forlorn sun
Forest green silhouettes the blue
As the colors embrace as one

The blues and grays dance across the sea
As golden leaves scent this story
The kiss of sea spray salts my face
As I drink it in, I share the glory

Rays of gold fan across the sea
As the date is parted by the setting sun
The kiss of night touches my face
As I drink it in, the day is done

❖

On Seeing Heaven Tonight

❖

Lights interfere, Cloud crossed moon

Stars… Planets… Nothing…

Calm happens elsewhere!

Watcher patiently hopes for sight.

❖

Gateway

❖

Silky Universe

Gateway to the human soul

Forever endless

❖

Goodbye Dark Moon

❖

As the moonlight laughs

At the balcony of stars above,

Marble rocks and jutting trees

Taste the soft night.

Then dawn swallows the Earth.

Old dew returns to the clouds,

As morning stretches

Touching midday

❖

The Storm

❖

Dark lightning cursed the shoreline

Drowning wave burst wildly in air

Frightening sea cry doom

Thunder was the clouds message

❖

Earth

❖

Hers is delicious nectar

And round silky body

She's the key to life

She's home

❖

Ode to the Dragon

❖

Genesis created the Earth, and let us all be free
To live in peace and harmony, was how it was meant to be
Plant, beast and spirit, shared the Earth you see
For the sky, land and sea, were home to you and me

The sun shined across the land, and everything was fair
Together we sang and danced, and held each other dear
But clouds began to block the sun, and darkness felt so near
The way man began to treat us, caused us to shed a tear

Whether Nordic or African, each must share the blame
For they felt superior, and told us to be tame
Some of us listened, and some of us became game
But hardly a man felt remorse, or even a drop of shame

Although we want to stay, darkness begins to fall
I wonder if man will miss us, when eternity finally calls

❖

Special

"Words are all we have."
- Samuel Beckett

Miles to Go Before I Sleep

By Past Poetry Masters and Christopher P. Obert

❖

Some say the world will end in fire, some say in ice

Anticipating	Darkness visible
Seeing	Every man for himself
Believing	Things fall apart

The glory that was Greece and the grandeur that was Rome

Anticipating	A world he never made
Seeing	Human kind cannot bear very much reality
Believing	Each man kills the thing he loves

Had we but world enough and time

Anticipating	Black as hell, Dark as night
Seeing	Fear in a handful of dust
Believing	His reach exceeds his grasp

God moves in a mysterious way

Anticipating	Into each life some rain must fall
Seeing	Every dark cloud has a silver lining
Believing	Hope springs eternal

To keep the wolf from the door

Anticipating	Stone walls do not a prison make
Seeing	Words are cheap
Believing	The child is father of the man

The road less traveled

Anticipating	Truth is stranger than fiction
Seeing	Patience is a virtue
Believing	Not of an age, but for all time

❖

Poetry is Needed

By Past Poetry Masters and Christopher P. Obert

❖

Poetry is needed

To stink like a goat
To play with fire
To knit one's brow
To wet one's whistle
To see and be seen
To let sleeping dogs lie
To fall on evil days
To strike while the iron is hot

Poetry is needed to teach

Love is blind
No man is an island
A little learning is a dangerous thing
All that glitters is not gold
Ignorance is bliss

Poetry is needed to feel

As fresh as a rose
As busy as a bee
Remembrance of things past
Gilded monuments
Love at first sight

Poetry is needed to show

The ghastly crew
The marriage of true minds
Oh, what a tangled web we weave
In one ear and out the other
The proper study of mankind

❖

And Redcap Waits

❖

Amesbury Massachusetts Seventeen Ninety One
Cemetery on the hill, where the deed was done
At a freshly dug grave, there the two did meet
One stood at the head, the other at the feet

They stared at each other without saying a word
Quiet enough to hear heartbeats, but not a one was heard
The air was still and cold that dark night
The glow of the stars their only light

One dressed in splendor, the other dressed in rags
Each eyeing the other like two opposing stags
They looked and looked and looked some more
Each knowing the other came through Hell's door

The one at the head, no more than a few days old
The other four hundred and seven years, so I am told.
The older of the two was the first to speak
Of which I will now… will now repeat

I'd knew you'd come, I heard the Gabriel Ratchets cry
Be gone foolish Hameh for I cannot die
Your strength and cunning are not up to your task
Be gone foolish Hameh, I will not again ask

The younger specter stood there silent and still
Looked down at the grave in the cemetery on the hill
Then he slowly raised his head and their eyes met
He had no fear of the older demon's threat

Lamiae, Nosferatu… I know you too
But I will bring you death, for there is nothing I can't do.
I was created for this one and only task
Surrender… Now, for I will not again ask!

You have wasted courage my young friend
But it will be you destroyed in the end.
I keep death in my pocket, my foot upon his neck
When I let him loose it will end your little trek.

To end man's journey you have the strength
You've done this many times I know the length
Your power strikes the eye this much is true
But tonight you will not deliver death, death will find you

Both were terrifying, irresistible, wicked and cold
Both knew and respected the other's talents, let it be told
Each walked only for one reason, to hear the death cries
Each knew the pain and horror of the sunrise

Neither could see the beauty of the land or sea or gulls
Both of them walked in a placed paved with priest's skulls
Each knowing its blood was not out of harm's way
Each of them knowing one of them would die this day

The battle, long and violent, it was quite a sight…
After said and done, only one survived the night
No human being saw their deadly embrace
Only I; interrupted from my ghostly pace

❖

The Angel

By Christopher P. Obert based on a story by
Gabriel Garcia Marquez

❖

God, God, God... Life for the child was meant.
God, God, God... For I was Heaven sent.

Down, Down, Down... Down to Earth I go.
Down, Down, Down... Heavy the rain does flow.

Crash, Crash, Crash... In the mud I lie.
Crash, Crash, Crash... Is this the time I die?

Pain, Pain, Pain... Broken wings I bear.
Pain, Pain, Pain... Does no one really care?

Earth, Earth, Earth... Down to Terra I came.
Earth, Earth, Earth... This is not a game.

Life, Life, Life... For I completed my task.
Life, Life, Life... What of me, I ask.

Caged, Caged, Caged... They just poke and stare.
Caged, Caged, Caged... All I feel is fear.

Look, Look, Look… See what a wretched site.
Look, Look, Look… The people know they're right.

Cash, Cash, Cash… Come and see the beast.
Cash, Cash, Cash… They don't care in the least.

Sad, Sad, Sad… I am so alone.
Sad, Sad, Sad… I want to go back home.

Time, Time, Time… Weeks turn into years.
Time, Time, Time… No one sheds any tears.

Dream, Dream, Dream… All I do is wait.
Dream, Dream, Dream… Is this to be my fate?

Beg, Beg, Beg… I am now the pet.
Beg, Beg, Beg… My wings began to set.

Health, Health, Health… Life returns to me.
Health, Health, Health… Life I brought to thee.

Off, Off, Off… Fly to Heaven, I do.
Off, Off, Off… None of them ever knew!

❖

The Chores of Mother Nature

By Giovannina Obert and Christopher P. Obert

❖

The chores of Mother Nature
Are wondrous to behold.
Each season tells a story,
That always is retold.

Skies of blue, Rainbow bright
Sea of color, Majestic white
Winter, Spring, Summer and Fall
Mother Nature did it all!

❖

Your Dream

By Shari Obert

❖

Peaceful and calm - a place you can hide-
So soothing to leave the world behind.

With the close of a door the outside world dims;
Time is suspended, your life begins.

Inside are your dreams - your one true self-
Your mask, thrown away, gathers dust on the shelf.

Free and unfettered, the oppressive burden gone,
With wings outspread you fly into the dawn.

Soaring and gliding, the wind on your wings-
Though the freedom is fleeting oh, the comfort it brings.

Slowly descending - your time is now through;
The world calls you home - there is naught you can do.

You touch up your mask and place it back on;
Your freedom and dreams irrevocably gone.

Back into the world you go with a sigh;
You hold back the tears - they must not see you cry.

You hope and you pray you'll return once again,
Though you believe that you will, you are not sure quite when.

To this faith you must cling with your heart and your mind,
Of the place you adore, and the heaven you'll find.

❖

Notes:

When I was young I hated poems. I did not want to read them. I did not want to write them. Looking back I guess I just did not understand them. Today I enjoy poems and I am the author of a book of poetry. You may wonder what changed me. I believe it was two events. The first happened in 1975. I had to write two poems for my 7th grade English class. I kept putting if off, and putting it off, until it was due the next day. I told my mother that I had to write two poems before tomorrow's class. She sat me down at the kitchen table and helped me write two poems. She made it seem not so much like work, but fun. The two poems were good. I liked them and was proud of them. One of those poems, *The Chores of Mother Nature* is included in this book. After that, I tried to write my first solo poem. *Planets of War*, also included in this book, was that first poem. So things were starting to change. Writing poems was not as bad as I thought it would be.

The second thing to change my opinion of poetry was discovering the poetry book, *Reflections of a Watermelon Pickle*, for which this book is named in honor of. I cannot remember if the book is a compilation or written by one author, but I do remember how much fun I had reading the poems in it. The book was full of light verse-style poems. They were short, fun and silly, not at all like the long, boring old poems I had to read in English class. I found I could understand these poems. I also discovered that once the door to poetry had been opened there was no going back. I started to find other poems that I liked and to understand what poets were trying to say.

Today, whenever I hear someone say that he does not like poetry, I realize that they just don't get it. I understand that to say that you do not like poetry is a ridiculous statement. It is like saying that you don't like all music or all movies or all novels or all paintings. You never hear those statements, so why do you hear it about poetry? I believe it is because the speaker has not yet found his own style of poetry. Just as there are dozens of different styles of music, there are dozens of styles of poetry. My goal in this book is to expose the reader to a few of those styles and give some background on my reason for writing them. I hope that you may find one that you like so you can go exploring the world of poetry to find similar poems.

Currently, I myself am still discovering poetry. I am still exploring. There are many poems I have found that I do not like and many that I do like. There are poems that I understand completely and others that I don't understand at all. But that is now part of the fun. I can look at any poem, any quote, any work of literature and embrace it or not. It is my choice.

As I have learned more about poetry and writing in general, I have learned much. I have found out that as mankind has experienced the world, artists have blanketed us with music, colored us with paint and fed us with words. Poetry has been one of the best tools of these artists. Poetry is one of the oldest art forms and has been around for thousands of years. It has played a major role in the development of human language and communication. Because of this role, it could be said that poetry has had a profound effect on the human soul. As mankind has lived, laughed and loved, poetry has recorded these emotions. Through years of war and crisis, poetry has shown the carnage; during adventures and exploration, poetry has relayed the wonder. Poetry is true emotions and feelings recorded.

The motivation behind poetry can come from many sources, such as family and lovers, locations and events, or works of art. I have started working on a follow-up book to this one, and one of my poems that may be in it was motivated by two science-fiction/fantasy paintings, and another one was inspired by Egyptian hieroglyphics. As you read through this book, you will find that some of the poems in it were motivated by things like my wife and children, my home, nature and past loves. You never know when a feeing will make you write a poem or the other way around… a poem will spark a feeling.

I hope this book opens the door of poetry for you… enjoy the ride!

A Note on the Images

All of the images in this book, except the author's photo, were taken from the clipart package *Art Explosion 600,000* (Nova Development Corporation Copyright © 1995-98). I chose all of the images and believe that they enhance the feel of the book. This software is incredibility useful, easy to use and contains thousands of great images. I highly recommend it.

"It's like striking a match. Sometimes it lights."
- Neil Simon

People and Places

The Hill

The Hill is the name we gave for the place I grew up. It was a small section of Amesbury, Massachusetts comprised of a part of Elm Street and all of Atlantic Avenue. It is so much a part of me that it is still the only home I dream of. I hope that you like this poem because it is one of my favorites. It is written in *Free Verse* and is an *Ode* to my past and the home I grew up in.

Me

In the summer of 1995 I took a computer course at Northern Essex Community College, Haverhill, Massachusetts. One of my assignments was to do a project on the computer. I decided to create a book of my poems illustrated with my own computer graphics. While I was showing my work to my wife, Nancy, I asked her if I should include some new poems to add to the book. She said, "Sure, why not?" This poem is what I came up with. I wrote it in about an hour and quickly showed it to Nancy. She asked if I just wrote it and I said, "Yes". She told me that she liked my poetry and wished she could write. I will let you in on a secret - she can write! But I will always remember her telling me that she liked my work, and this made me start to think about writing a poetry book. This poem is also written in *Free Verse*. To me, free verse is one of the most fun poetry styles, because it allows the poet to be very free with his writing. This poem is also considered *Light Verse*. Light verse is poetry that, as the name implies, has a "light" subject matter. This style poem should be fun and comical to read.

Good-bye, My Friend

November 26, 2002 – my attempt at a Shakespearian toned poem. This poem was written for my best friend "Cook" who died in 1985. I love you buddy. I feel this is one of my best poems, if not my best. This poem is written in the form of a *Ballad*. Although I call this a Shakespearian poem, it is in it's tone only. It is not a Shakespearian Sonnet. This poem is more of an *Elegy*.

At Home (Strolling Through Time)

This poem is in honor of the City of Haverhill, Massachusetts. The idea for this poem came to me as I was looking through the book, *Images of America – Haverhill Massachusetts from Town to City*, by Patricia Trainor O'Malley. This "photo book" displayed many scenes of Haverhill through the years. These images transported me through time and this poem was my way of recording that journey. Although I consider Amesbury "home", Haverhill welcomed me and is the hometown for my children. It has always made me feel at home. This poem is written in *Heroic Couplet*, which has an aabbcc rhyming pattern. It is my goal to write more poems about the surrounding communities. I have been reading a lot of John Greenleaf Whittier's (1807-1892) poems. He is a Haverhill and Amesbury native and is a great poet. I especially like his poems, *The Captain's Well* and *In School Days*. It is fun to read poems that use names and locations that you know. I recommend that everyone should read the poetry of a local poet (as well as Whittier's poems).

Not Everyone Can Be a Poet

While I was working on this poetry book, I tried to come up with a really fantastic poem to add to my collection. No matter how hard I tried nothing worked, nothing flowed, nothing! The only thing that stayed in my mind was this poem. I feel that this poem is kind of childish sounding but the sentiment is still very true. Whenever a poem's theme is about poetry or a poet, the poem is called an *Ars Poetica*. This poem is written in the style of a *Ballad*. A ballad is a poem that tells a story of recent events, lost loves or supernatural events.

Chris' Law

I wrote this *One-liner* in 1977. It is hard to explain, but I think you can figure it out. There once was this girl that I would do anything for… even if it tore me apart. I had to realize that I must live for me and not her! I have never gotten over her, and she still lives in my heart. Thankfully, I found another girl that I could love and live for, just as she loves and lives for me!!! (Note that *Chris' Law* is not a statement but a question!)

On a Corner Street

This poem is a continuation of *Chris' Law*. It refers to the same girl and how when your heart is broken it takes a long time to fix. This poem is what I call a *Snip-it*. Snip-its are very short *Free Verse* poems. These poems are short like *Haiku*s but do not have to follow any rules. Famous quotes or one-liners could also be considered snip-its. Generally, I feel a snip-it is any short collection of words that tell a larger story than would be expected from the number of words. There are companies that sell magnetic words that you can arrange on your refrigerator and web-sites that can help you to create short snip-it type poems using similar methods. Give them a try.

My Wife and Children

December and You

I wrote this poem for my wife Nancy for our Fifth Anniversary (1986). It is the first true love poem I ever wrote. I wrote half of it at home, then I brought it to work (at AT&T) to finish the other half. This poem is a form of a *Heroic Couplet.* This is a fun style of poem with an aabbcc type rhyming pattern. I ended this Heroic Couplet poem with an abcb rhyme.

An Open Letter to Y3K

12/31/1999 – This *Letter* was written for my wife Nancy. The sentiment behind this letter is so true. I had been dreaming of the year 2000 all my life. Being a fan of science fiction, and a lover of science, that day was so important. But as the day neared, I could only think of Nancy. After writing this letter, I e-mailed it to my wife. When a poem is written to someone in a letter form, it is sometimes called an *Epistle Poem.* Epistle Poems date back to the days of the Bible, but I don't think anyone back then ever thought of an e-mail epistle!

A Picture

I wrote this poem many years ago. I like this poem. I have, however, thought about rewriting it many times, I just have never gotten around to doing it. I think if I changed the beginning and lengthened the poem it could be better. The idea behind this poem came to me as I was cleaning collected junk out of my wallet and looked at a photo of my wife, Nancy. This *Stanza* has a simple rhyming pattern with a loose arrangement of lines making it a *Quasi-Stanzaic* poem.

The Lady and the Children

November 2004 - written for my wife Nancy and our children, Shari and Jason. This poem was one of the hardest I have ever written. I got the idea for this poem after reading Edgar Allen Poe's poem, *A Valentine.* My poem has a simple abab rhyming pattern ending with an ii rhyme, yet it, like Poe's, contains a secret message. To find the hidden name of *The Lady* you must circle the first letter in the list line. Next, circle the second letter in the second line. Continue to do this, third letter third line, forth letter forth line and so on to the end of the poem. These letters will spell out the name! The task of creating a flowing poem that uses an abab rhyming pattern and that has the letters of the secret message imbedded within it made this poem very difficult to write.

Please Don't Ever Go

In addition to writing poems, I also write songs. I come up with a tune and try to find words that fit. I never write the words then try to come up with the music. This is one of these songs. This song/poem is part three in a group of three. The first I wrote many, many years ago for an old girlfriend. The title was *Not the Same Anymore*. There was a line in it that stated "Living with her was always a chore" describing the problems we had while dating. The second song/poem was titled *Love You Lots*. It was dedicated to the girl I dated next. It had the line "Loving you isn't a chore" showing the new hope I had. It ended with the line "I Love You Lots – Till the very end…" Well guess what, it did end. The next girl I dated was Nancy, the girl I ended up marrying. *Please Don't Ever Go* was written in the 1980's and is dedicated to Nancy and the end of a line of broken hearts. This poem is written similar to an *Isometric Stanza*. I personally call my song/poems "musical stanzas."

The Unending Love Game

This poem started out life as a *Snip-it*. I then used its opening line, "Two children happened to me" to create a *Pantoum* style poem. A pantoum has no defined length but uses an abab rhyming pattern. The pantoum also uses a repetition of two lines from each stanza to the next. The twenty lines are as follows: 1, 2, 3, 4 – 2, 6, 4, 8 – 6, 10, 8, 12 – 10, 14, 12, 16 – 17, 3, 19, 1. The poem ends with the opening line.

"All bad poetry springs from genuine feeling."
- Oscar Wilde

"Words are like water – the assumption being that it moves in any direction."
- Bernard Malamud

Thoughts and Emotions

Stephanie – Broken Dream Girl

One day, in the late 1980's, my nieces came over my house. They brought a friend with them, Stephanie. She was a very beautiful girl and I was very impressed with her. Although she was very nice I could tell that someday she could unknowingly break some young man's heart. At the same time, I was working on a song/poem and needed a girl's name. Her name just seemed to fall into place. I do not remember ever seeing her again, so I never told her that she has a musical stanza out there... This musical stanza is written in a *Quasi-stanzaic* form. A quasi-stanzaic poem is a *Stanza* with a loose grouping of lines and paragraphs.

Rake the Dead

I got the idea for this late 1980's song/poem from my friend Alex Vannett. He had this saying, "Rake the Dead". He thought the line sounded awful, but he would say it all the time. Whenever I heard the line, I thought of the way the media attacks people, especially after they have died. It is as if they are just waiting for death or bad news so that they can attack these people. I started to think, "The media people will get what they sow." That is how I came up with the idea behind this musical stanza. The woman in this story uses all the dirt she can find to help her career, but after she is gone, they attack her! This musical stanza is written in a *Quasi-stanzaic* form.

Seafarer's Cabin

This is one of my Owl's Head Poems. My family and I have vacationed at Owl's Head, Maine for many years. Every year we visit a cabin owned by David and Sheila, friends of our family. While there, I love to sit and take in the view. It is a great place to write poetry. This poem is written in *Isometric stanza*.

Before it's Too Late

It is funny how a few words can hold so much emotion. You experience this every time you hear a line from a song or movie that instantly transports you to another time, another place, filling you with a memory. This *Snip-it* is one of my favorites because it takes me to moments in my past that I wish I could relive. This poem speaks not of being sorry for love but sorry for the things that were left unsaid.

The Unsaid Word

This *One-liner* is also one of my favorites. It continues on with the theme of *Before It's Too Late*. It definitely tells a bigger story than you would expect from eight words. Obviously, the unsaid word between these two friends is "Love." How they deal with these new emotions is anyone's guess.

Timeless

What can I write in this book to make love easier, more understandable? I can't think of anything, I just hope that my poems somehow speak to you and relay truth. This *Snip-it* contains one of my favorite lines, "Heaven is beyond time." I feel it is one of the best lines I have ever written.

Music

This short *Snip-it* poem addresses the sentiment, "Those that can't act, direct." The subject of this poem can't sing, so the person finds expression in the playing of the piano. Writing poetry is another example of how someone can find a voice for those inner feelings.

Desperation

This poem is a little confusing to read, but it was meant that way. This *Snip-it* tries to express the feeling of desperation. Logic fails, dark emotions run wild and dreams are eclipsed.

Past Memories

This *Snip-it* is an *Ode* to the sadness of old love letters. Love letters could be considered a type of poetry. The message held within speaks directly to the heart.

Oblivious

This *Snip-it* is dedicated to all those oblivious to the love around them. When I was in high school there was always a girl that I had feelings for, but she did not know that I existed. No matter how hard I tried, I could not get her to see how I felt. I would wonder how she could not see how I felt. The thought never occurred to me that I may have been blind to the fact that someone may have had feelings for me and struggled to gain my attention.

Memories

8/18/04 I think this *Snip-it* is one of my best. It relates to the statement, "Time heals all wounds." The only question is, how much time?

Snowflakes – On the River of Time

This poem partly came to me early one morning as I was lying in bed half awake. I got up, puttered around for a while, and then sat to write it down. We were having company that day and I was still sitting upstairs trying to work the poem out on paper as they were arriving. I finally came down when my mother showed up. I met her at the door and she told me that she was sorry that she was late, but she had woken up that morning with a poem in her head and just had to write it down! This poem is written in *Free Verse*. Most of the time I write in free verse, but I am trying to purposely write in other poetic forms.

"No tears in the writer, no tears in the reader."
- Robert Frost

"There is no advice to give young poets."
- Pablo Neruda

Faith

God and Religion

This poem was written in June of 1987. I was sitting on my back deck doing U.S. History homework for a college course I was taking at NECC. My mind wondered for a moment and I glanced at the sun reflecting off of my wedding ring. The poem came to me all at once, as if someone whispered it into my ear. It is the only poem that has come to me that way. It is also the first poem that I ever submitted for others to read. I sent it in to *Poetry.com* and it won their Editor's Choice Award for June 2004. It was included in *Poetry.com's* compilation book, *The Silent Journey*, distributed in July 2004.

Chris' Prayer

I wrote this in 1999. I wanted something special to pray to God, a prayer of my own. I thought that if I could pray something, not just lines that I memorized, but something from my heart, it would be more meaningful. If you think about it, all prayers and hymns are like poems. Their only role is to convey many strong feelings in a compact form. I think we all should have our own prayer, maybe more than one!

God the Artist

When trying to put these poems into some kind of order I found myself thinking, "Where should *God the Artist* go?" I knew that I wanted to have a section on Love, but did it belong there or maybe in a section on Sex? I decided that I would put it in the Faith section. The reason for this is simple. Most people do not think of God when they think about sex. Why is that? God created all the parts! All the emotions! I believe sex, when coupled with love, is a beautiful thing. Just ask God the artist… One last note about this poem - this is the only *Calligram* poem in this book. Calligrams (also called *Emblematic Poems*) are poems that are written in a particular shape relating to the poem's subject. Can you see God's Eye in this *Snip-it*?

Nature's King

Life and Death, as well as the changing of the Seasons, are the themes of this *Snip-it*. This poem is my way of stating my belief that just as the seasons change, so do our lives. As surely as spring follows winter, a new life follows death.

To Touch the Universe

I believe that each of us is connected. Everything that you and I do affects people, unknown to us, on the other side of the world. Likewise, the events on the Earth affect the rest of the universe. This *Snip-it* builds off of my poem *Me*, especially the line, "I am a part of the Universe and it is a part of me."

Crucified

I hope that you do not feel like I am preaching to you with my Faith based poems. I do not want to force my beliefs onto anyone. I just want to relay the wonder I see in the world and its people to the readers. I do believe in God but I also believe in us. I believe faith is much more important than religion. This *Snip-it*, although it seems to refer to Jesus, is also about everyone that works for a better life and a better world.

"A complete poem is one where an emotion has found its thought and the thought has found the words."
- Robert Frost

"Everyone has talent. What is rare is the courage to follow the talent into the dark place where it leads."
- Erica Jong

War and Liberty

Planets of War

I wrote this poem in 1975 just for the fun of it. It is the first poem I ever wrote on my own. I can remember sitting in the Amesbury Middle School Library working on this poem. I have never been happy with two of the lines in the poem: "Even with their certain fate,/They never try to change that date./For it eventually must come/To worlds that are so dumb." Originally the line was "Even with their certain fate,/They never try to change that fate./For as it must come/to worlds that are so dumb." I like my original version better but felt the second version was more appropriate English. I still think that those lines could somehow be better. This poem is an *Elegy* written in *Heroic Couplet.*

America

I am truly grateful that I am an American. I love this country very much and pray every day that I am worthy of citizenship. I also pray that the United States works to be a true light for the rest of the world. God Bless America! This poem is written as a *Snip-it.*

When Will We Learn

Waste. What a horrible word, especially when it deals with human lives. Whenever I read about war I cannot help but think that although wars may be fought for righteous reasons, they nevertheless are a waste of lives! I feel that this *Snip-it* is one of my better ones.

Eternal Dream

Eternal Dream is a continuation of *When Will We Learn*. I often wonder what the souls of the dead think of us. How they must scream from beyond, trying to tell us not to follow in their footsteps. But do any of us listen? This poem also started out as a *Snip-it*. I took some of the wording from the old snip-it and wrote a new poem in the form of a *Villanelle*. A villanelle is a 19 line poem with an aba rhyming series. The poem reuses the first and third lines of the poem at different locations in the poem. The 19 lines looks like this: 1, 2, 3 – 4, 5, 1 – 7, 8, 3 – 10, 11, 1 – 13, 14, 3 – 16, 17, 1, 3. *Eternal Dream* is special to me because it is the first poem of mine to be accepted for publication by a magazine. The magazine, *Space and Time*, publishes science fiction, fantasy and horror poetry and short features. The issue containing *Eternal Dream* will be printed sometime in 2005. I recommend that you check out this magazine.

The Words of War

I wanted to try and write another poem about war. I went to a dictionary and looked for words that I could use to supplement my own. As I looked through the listing of words, I was very surprised at how many words in the dictionary could be used. I guess because war is such a huge part of mankind's mentality, we devote many words to it. This poem, if you could call it a poem, is a *Word List*. The goal behind this poem is to make the reader consider how many issues can start conflicts which lead down the road to war. You may have noticed that ten of the words are in **bold** print. I feel that these ten words are the biggest reasons behind most wars. What ten words would you pick?

"Poetry is the art of understanding what it is to be alive."
- Archibald MacLeish

"To a poet, silence is an acceptable response, even a flattering one."
- Colette

Nature

Dreaming of Spring

This poem was originally two *Snip-it* poems. The first was called *The Seasons* (first four lines). The second was called *Dreaming of Spring* (last four lines). As I was putting the poems into this book, I put these two poems on the same page. As I read over the page I found that the two poems fit nicely together to make one better longer poem. The only problem I saw was the use of leaves twice, but I thought that this use was OK. The first section is remembering the past year while the second section is the cold now... dreaming of spring.

The Harmony of the Birch

This is another of my Owl's Head Poems. This Stanza has three recurring lines creating a pattern. Because the poem's lines are of different lengths, it is called *Heterometric*. This poem speaks of the harmony of nature and asks why we can't follow nature's teaching and live in peace.

The Wind Chime

This *Isometric Stanza* poem is also an Owl's Head Poem. It slowly flowed out of me onto the paper as I sat watching a wind chime blowing in the breeze. I tried to have the poem be short but musical, similar to the sound emanating from the wind chime.

Across the Sea

This is another of my Owl's Head Poems. It is written in the form of a *Ballad*. This poem contains two of my best lines: "As the rusted anchor whispers its story" and "The kiss of sea spray salts my face." I like the way this poems flows but I feel there is something missing. Maybe in time I will figure it out.

On Seeing Heaven Tonight

When I was a child I wanted to grow up and be an astronomer. I loved science and science fiction and was forever looking up. It is to be expected that some of my poems deal with science and nature. This poem speaks of the frustration every night sky viewer goes through... praying for clear skies! This poem is a *Snip-it*.

Gateway

This poem is in the form of a *Haiku*. A haiku is an Oriental verse form. It is constructed of three lines. The first and third have five syllables and the second line uses seven syllables. I have not written many Haikus. To tell you the truth, I do not like most Haikus. I find them too restrictive. But at the same time I have to give them credit, since they force the writer to be quick and to the point, something I like in my poetry.

Goodbye Dark Moon

8/20-22/04

This poem also started out as two *Snip-its*, one named *Night* and one named *Goodbye Dark Moon*. I combined them into one poem the same way I did *Dreaming of Spring*. As you can see, writing snip-its is not only fun but can lead to other longer poems. Snip-its can also give you an idea that you can build off of, as I did with *The Unending Love Game* and *Eternal Dreams*.

The Storm

This *Snip-it* was fun to write. I have always loved storms… the blacks and grays and, of course, the lightning. This is a great snip-it that could be expanded into a much longer poem. What do you think? This book contains many snip-its which could be used to create other poems. Pick the one you like best and give it a shot…

Earth

This *Snip-it* is inspired by the Gaia Theory. This theory, named after the Greek goddess of the Earth, was developed by James Lovelock and Lynn Margulis. They believe that life and the Earth evolved tightly together, creating a single entity. This entity, Gaia (life and Earth), is self regulating and works so closely together that it acts as if it were alive. The more I study this theory, the more I find it to be true.

Ode to the Dragon

November 2004. This poem is a *Heroic Couplet* which uses an aabbcc rhyme pattern. It uses no set number of syllables in each line. The poem is my way of pointing out the *Irony* that we dream of animals long gone (like the dinosaurs) or the ones that never were (the Dragons), while at the same time destroying those still here. The title is a *Metaphor* for endangered species.

"If I feel physically as if the top of my head were taken off,
I know that is poetry."
- Emily Dickinson

Special

Miles to Go Before I Sleep

By Past Poetry Masters and Christopher P. Obert

July 2004 - I only wrote three words in this poem - anticipating, believing and seeing. The remainder of the poem is a compilation of famous lines from other poets, such as Geoffrey Chaucer, William Shakespeare, John Skelton, T.S. Eliot and Henry Wadsworth Longfellow. These poets are masters of their art and I am very far away from their level of talent. My goal was to try and use some of their famous lines to tell a story. If I succeeded, this story will tell the tale that the human race is complicated. Although mankind (and woman-kind) has an evil side, we also have a divine side. We do not have to end in destruction, but are capable of wondrous creations. It will take time and we need to be patient. With God's help, and by working together, we can make it. But we have a long way to go. This poem is the first in my "Masters" series. It is written in *Heterometric* form.

Poetry is Needed

By Past Poetry Masters and Christopher P. Obert

August 2004 - This poem is the second in my "Masters" series. This poem is compiled of famous lines from other great poets. I only wrote the "Poetry is needed" title lines. After compiling *Miles to Go Before I Sleep*, I quickly realized that there were so many great lines found in poetry that I could compile many more poems from them. This poem was my next attempt. My goal in this poem was to put an interesting group of famous lines into one hodgepodge of ideas that somehow flowed and looked appealing. If I succeeded, after reading the many great lines, you will have a better understanding of how poetry touches many emotions. This poem is written in *Quasi-stanzaic*. In these two poems, *Poetry is Needed* and *Miles to Go Before I Sleep*, can you identify the poets who wrote the lines?

And Redcap Waits

October 2004 - This poem takes some explaining. The poem is the story (told by a ghost) of the meeting of a Vampire and a Hameh. As you know, a vampire is a supernatural being that is a walking corpse. It survives by drinking a human's blood, thus killing them. However, this vampire made the mistake of letting some of the blood of the victim touch the ground. There is an ancient Arabian legend of a Hameh, which is also a supernatural being that is created out of the blood of a murder victim. Its only purpose is to seek revenge and kill the murderer by drinking his blood. This poem is the story of what would happen if the two met. I do not know who would win such a duel, so I leave it to the reader to guess the answer. I first had the idea of the two demons meeting after reviewing the book, *Monsters Who's Who*, by Dulan Barber. I then decided that I wanted the poem to be similar in style to, *Twas the Night Before Christmas*. My poem tells a story, not of someone watching Santa, but of someone watching a vampire. I wanted the poem to have a classic feel to it so I did some research on words and sayings that I could use in the poem. I found that "Lamiae" and "Nosferatu" are other names for vampire. I also found that "Gabriel Ratchets," old English mythological creatures, were restless souls whose cries announced the approach of death. Borrowing from Steven King, who uses local locations in his stories, I used Amesbury as the location of the encounter. When writing this poem, I really wanted to write something special and add a little history and culture to this classic encounter, so I included references to some famous quotes in the poem:

The world is all the richer for having the devil in it, so long as we keep our foot upon his neck. - William James

No notice is taken of a little evil, but when it increases it strikes the eye. - Aristotle

Do not seek death. Death will find you. - Dag Hammarskjöld

We may not pay Satan reverence, for that would be indiscreet, but we can at least respect his talents. - Mark Twain

I have a horror of the sunsets, they're so romantic, so operatic. - Marcel Proust

Hell is paved with priest's skulls. - John Chrysostom

Lastly, I want to give an explanation for the title of this poem. "Redcap", another English mythological creature, is a dwarf that lingers in the shadows at the scenes of violent encounters. As legend states, he wears a cap that gets its color from blood. Redcap is constantly looking for fresh blood to dip his cap in. Because this poem has an aabbcc rhyming pattern it is a *Heroic Couplet* but it could also be interpreted as a *Ballad*, written with an aabbcc rhyme pattern. The poem is also best described as a combination of *Ode* and *Elegy.* I believe this poem is the longest I have ever written so it could be considered my *Epic*.